The Table of Phinneas Fable

A STORY FOR YOU FROM
Big Math for Little Kids™

Carole Greenes   Robert Balfanz   Herbert P. Ginsburg
Illustrated by Jamie Smith

DALE SEYMOUR PUBLICATIONS
Pearson Learning Group

National Science Foundation

This material is based on work supported by the National Science Foundation under Grant No. ESI-9730683. Any opinions, findings, conclusions, or recommendations expressed here are those of the authors and do not necessarily reflect the views of the National Science Foundation.

ISBN 0-7690-2869-1

1-800-321-3106
www.pearsonlearning.com

The pasta maker,
Phinneas Fable,
Cut some dough on his
Big kitchen table.

He made different shapes
With the pasta dough.
Then he put the shapes
In a nice neat row.

1

First came a circle.
Then came a square.
He made the pattern
With very great care.

"What shapes come next?"
He thought to himself,
As he took more dough
From the kitchen shelf.

3

"Next there's a circle.
Then there's a square.
I love the pattern
Of shapes I prepare."

Phinneas Fable
Rolled out some more dough.
He cut lots of shapes
To make a new row.

Square, circle, triangle
Are all made of dough.
Square, circle, triangle
Are all in a row.

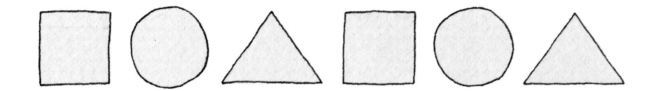

"Look at the pattern
And see if you know
Which shape belongs at
The end of the row."

"It's a triangle
Did I hear you say?
You are right!
Hip hip hooray!"

8

Phinneas Fable
Rolled out some more dough.
He cut lots of shapes
To make a new row.

Square, square, triangle
Are all made of dough.
Square, square, triangle
Are all in a row.

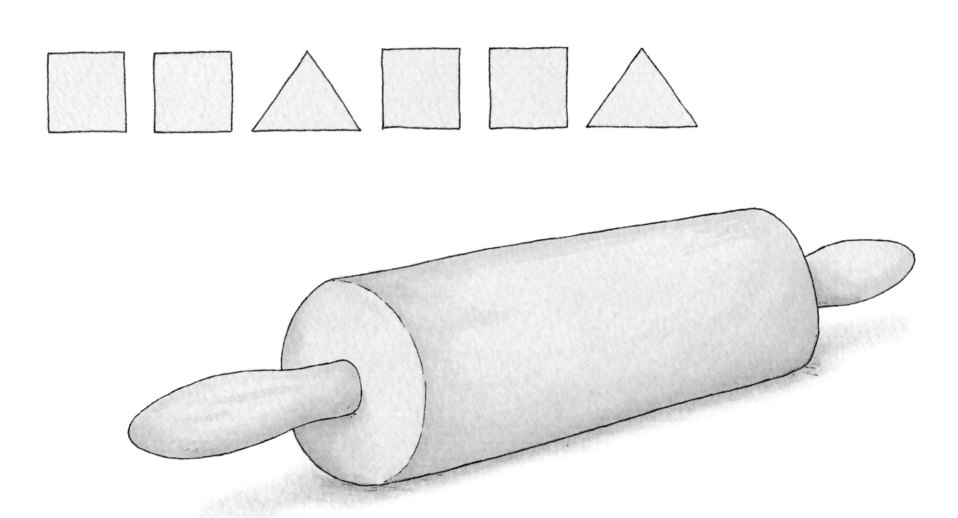

"Look at this pattern
And see if you know
Which shape belongs next
In the pasta row."

"It's a square
Did I hear you say?
You are right!
Hip hip hooray!"

Phinneas Fable
Rolled out some more dough.
He cut lots of shapes
To make a new row.

"Oops," said Phinneas.
"The pattern I see
Is missing a shape.
What could it be?"

Here are some patterns
For you to do.
Just find what's missing
And name the shapes too!

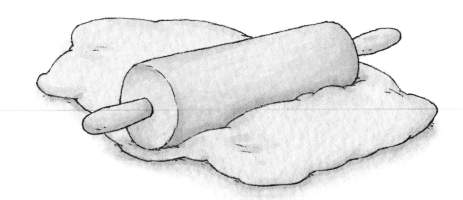

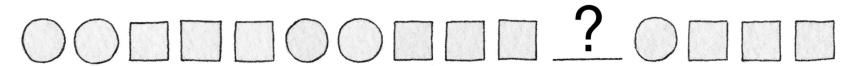

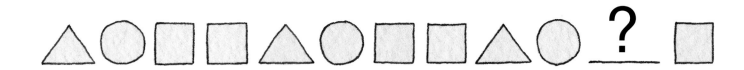